Secrets

To Creating Passive Income

& becoming financially free

(updated for 2010)

A Books To Believe In
Publication

by
EJ Thornton
&
John Clark Craig

A Books To Believe In Publication

Original copyright date,
first printing 2008

Proudly Published in the USA by
Thornton Publishing, Inc
17011 Lincoln Ave. #408
Parker, CO 80134

Phone: 303.794.8888
Fax: 720.863.2013

RevenueBeyond.com

ISBN: 0-9801941-9-9

2010

This is the third printing of *Secrets to Creating Passive Income* and the authors have revised this book to address the constantly changing conditions of the Internet, laws that have changed, companies that have been created or gone out of business, etc.

The world is constantly changing, and with each change, a new opportunity is created... are you watching?

The trends are favoring those who can see these opportunities and capitalize on them. That being said, the basic information and premise of this book is timeless.

The authors sincerely hope this information serves you well...

To Everyone's Financial Freedom

***

There is enough To Go Around!

Table of Contents

MAKE YOUR MONEY WORK FOR YOU

YOUR NEEDS, YOUR GOAL

All the breaks you need in life wait within your imagination.

Imagination is the workshop of your mind, capable of turning mind energy into accomplishment and wealth.

~Napoleon Hill
author of "Think & Grow Rich"

Introduction to Financial Freedom

Most people, when asked what they "do for a living" respond with a description of their 'Active Income'* source - their job, profession or basically, their main source of income as if how you generated your money defined you.

Wouldn't you rather answer that question with a description of what you 'love' to do? Financial freedom is about freeing you from having to go to work to meet your expenses, allowing you to chose to spend your time at something you love. *Maybe that is still work,* but it'll be work you choose to do. Maybe it'll be the volunteer *work* you've always wanted to do. Maybe it'll be spending time with others inspiring them to become financially free also so that you can go on trips to fantastic places together now - not when you're too old to enjoy it!

*__Active Income__ is whatever you are doing to create your paycheck today. For most people it is a job with an hourly wage or annual salary. Either way, it is a trade, your time for their money.

So, what is the definition of "Financial Freedom?"

The description that makes the most sense is the simplest one:

"Financial freedom is achieved when you get your passive income to exceed your expenses."

Fine then, what is "Passive Income?"

"Passive Income" is defined many ways.

The IRS defines passive income as ***"income generated by an activity in which the taxpayer does not materially participate."***

Passive Income is not time dependent.

Passive Income works for you, not the other way around.

Passive Income will require some activity and attention, but the time involved will be minimal compared to the returns. You get to determine how much time and when you spend it.

True Passive Income is something that you can walk away from and it still pays you.

Passive income has the ability to multiply, without limit, the use of your time, effort and energy.

Some good examples of passive income are:

- royalties on a book
- income from an e-book
- interest income on money in the bank
- rental income on an investment property
- stock dividends
- affiliate commissions
- multi-level marketing structures
- digital product sales
- referral bonuses
- consulting
- teaching / tuition
- raising fish, plants, pets
- online advertising commissions
- advertising for others using your property
- vending machine income
- advertsing on websites
- selling of used products on auction sites
- subscriptions or memberships

About the Authors

EJ Thornton

When EJ was creating her course "Seven Ways To Make Everyday a Payday" as a tele-course, she rediscovered how many terrific ways there are to make money in addition to whatever else you might be doing at the moment (i.e. your job, etc).

She's written three books to help authors look past book sales and into multiple revenue streams to not only promote their books, but to ***get paid*** to promote their books. All the very successful authors will tell you this is the way to go from moderately successful to enormously successful as an author!*

So she decided to apply these techniques to help the average person in their daily work. She's used it and it works. She's taught it, and the people who've worked these ideas have made lots of extra money.

* Revenue Beyond Royalties **ISBN: 1-932344-39-X** RevenueBeyond.com
Basics of Profitable Publishing, **ISBN: 1-932344-50-0** ThorntonPublishing.com
Seven Ways To Make Everyday a Payday, **RevenueBeyond.com**
Advanced Book Marketing, ISBN: 0-9820838-6-6, **AdvancedBookMarketing.com**

JOHN CLARK CRAIG

John has authored more than a dozen successful books for Microsoft Press and O'Reilly Media.* He found out that you can actually do the things you love while collecting passive income from book royalties! In other words, he was financially free.

John, also is a brilliant inventor. He now owns his own company - LucidLights, LLC. He is actively creating the lucrative company of his dreams! He can do so with full time and with confidence, because he knows his bills are handled with his passive income streams.

John increased his expenses by getting married recently, so now he has to increase his passive income to exceed the expenses of his new larger family.

That is why EJ & John decided to bring this book to you! They want you to join them living the 'free' life!

* Visual Basic 2005 Cookbook **ISBN: 0596101775** John Craig & Tim Patrick
Visual Basic 6.0 Developers Workshop, **ISBN: 157231883X** John Craig
LucidLights, **LucidLights.net**
LucidBrake**, LucidBrake.com**

Our Wish for Our Readers...

Most people talk about *'living the good life.'* Meaning they have all sorts of gadgets, gizmos and stuff! Most likely they've had to pay for that stuff with credit and now find that they have a lot of toys, but have to work long hours and/or extra jobs just to pay for all that stuff!

There's an old saying that, "The one who dies with the most toys - wins!" But we'd like to replace that common-place saying with one that makes a lot more sense, **"The one that gets free first - wins!" It's time to start talking about *'living the free life!'***

Every one of the financial gurus will tell you where to invest or how to grow your money so that you can be financially free. We've listened to many great ones like you probably have. But for the most part, they only tell you their one way to create passive income and the way they describe usually makes ***them*** the most money! Don't get us wrong, this is capitalism at its greatest and we wish them the best because there is a lot of good information out there.

Just for the record, we do want to ***sell*** you this book - it helps us. We also want to show you dozens and dozens of ways that you can make passive income starting right now. We also want to help you create a plan to become financially free - and do it in diversified ways, such that even if the economy dips in one area (such as stocks or real estate), you're still building toward that wonderful day when the alarm rings and you get to choose whether or not to go to work. If you go to work, it's because you ***want*** to, not because you have to.

This is our way of creating a win/win proposition.

The "Hours For Money" Model Does not Create Financial Freedom

Most people trade their time for money.

That is what an hourly wage is. The main problem with hourly wages, (even terrific hourly wages), is that there is a finite amount of them in any given day, week, month, year or lifetime.

There are 8760 hours in any year. A typical work year is 40*52 (or 2080) hours that you can get paid for. Roughly 23% of your year is devoted entirely to someone else's dream. You'll never become financially free working for someone else's dream - you need your own!

What if you used the remaining 77% of the year to develop some passive income streams, so that ultimately, when you are financially free, you can spend 100% of your time fulfilling your life's dream? ***"BUT WAIT!"*** you say, ***"77% of my time isn't available! I have to sleep, you know!"*** And to that we say, passive income isn't time dependent. We love to bounce out of bed every morning, run to the computers to find out how much money we made while we slept! Passive Income isn't time dependent, so you can get every hour of every day working for you!

So, it's time now, to spend some time developing the passive income streams you'll need to pay your expenses so that you can do whatever it is that you please!

You may already have developed some passive income streams. If so, you'll look at them in completely new way - as keys to your financial freedom!

"It Takes Money To Make Money" Is a Myth

Most of the up-front investment in these ideas is going to be your time and creativity. You'll have to do the writing or the analysis or the research. Once you decide on a stream of passive income, it might start to produce without you ever spending a penny on it and be in profits from day one. We have had several streams of passive income start that way - books start that way, affiliate programs usually start that way, freelance article writing usually starts that way and the list goes on.

However, some of these ideas do take money, and if you don't have the money for an idea that you know could work, ***there are options!***

There is no need for feelings of frustration because something you'd like to do has some start-up costs associated with it and you can't comfortably spend the money or simply don't have it. Somebody has it! And if you make the deal sweet enough, they'll loan it to you to get started!

Find someone you know who has money and can afford to live without the amount you need for a while. In other words, find someone for whom this amount of money is non-essential. What you need is "patient money."

Ask them for a short term loan. Offer them a great interest rate. Better yet, make them a partner in your idea - to a comfortable and reasonable point. If you need someone else's money to get started making money of your own, you need to start out being very generous!

These ideas are designed to create 'Win/Win' situations. If your lender is already financially free, then they should be able to evaluate the deal and decide if it works for them. If they are not financially free yet, explain the value of creating short term passive income through a loan to you. After you read this book, that will become a very easy thing to do.

The "System" is designed to make the 'rich get richer.' So, creating win/win situations with someone wealthy, will give you an ally helping you achieve your goal.

How the Rich Do it!

Remember, that many people who have achieved extreme riches tell similar stories which include these aspects:

- They had a great idea.
- They assembled a great team (of people smarter than them) to pull it off. Very few of these mega-moguls did it alone.
- They followed the advice of and associated with people who already were where they wanted to be.
- They never let anyone steal their dream.

Most people don't understand someone who wants to do something extraordinary (like getting financially free) and usually will try to shoot holes in the new ideas, because they don't understand them. "Dream Stealing" is common and can be extremely discouraging, unless you know how to defend against it.

Rich people keep their eye on the prize and don't let themselves be discouraged by 'well-meaning' people with free opinions. What must be looked at when receiving 'unsolicited advice' is whether or not the advice-giver is where you want to be. If they are, then their advice is probably valid, if they are not, then (no offense to them), but they don't know that they don't know. Their advice should be weighed only after passing this litmus test.

Rich people usually don't care what other people think about them. They aren't being cavalier or stand-offish, they just know they can't let other people's opinions influence them.

You're probably aware of the "80/20 rule," where 80% of the work is done in 20% of the time (or by 20% of the people). The rich live in about a 99%/1% world, where 99% percent of the wealth is controlled by 1% of the people. The "System" is designed that way and they think differently than the 99% who aren't financially free. Because they can maintain that kind of intellectual freedom, they can achieve financial freedom.

A shift has to occur in you, if you want to become financially free. First, decide you're worth it. Next decide you're going to go for it. Third, don't let anyone else convince you that your freedom isn't worth working for!

Follow the model of the rich and realize you never have to do it alone! It isn't 'lonely at the top,' it's just a new set of people, not better, not smarter, just a different attitude - they are free. Being free can really shift your perspective! Once you understand this, many of the psychological barriers you have against 'the rich' (and you becoming one of 'them') vanish and creating wealth becomes much easier - on so many levels!

Do Us A Favor...

Get a notebook and your favorite pen and be ready to write down ANY idea that comes to you in this next section. Take one paragraph at a time, and if an idea sparks in you, write it down!

DO NOT EDIT YOURSELF RIGHT NOW!

This next section is about brainstorming and during a brainstorming session, no idea is a bad one. You can always cross it off the list later, but you may never recapture that moment of inspiration. So instead of letting a potentially good idea go, write it down. If you write down an idea you think is crazy, that's okay, it might not be crazy in a month or two. Just trust the moment, and let your creative juices flow.

Take several deep breaths to focus your concentration on yourself, your ideas and your commitment to your financially free future!

Idea Fest

"An idea that is developed and put into action is more important than an idea that exists only as an idea."

~Buddha

The Value of an Opinion

Opinions turn into products!

Open your notebook and write each of the questions in this chapter on a separate piece of paper. Write down anything that comes to mind immediately, and keep the notebook close during the next few days to write down whatever ideas pop up in your day-to-day experiences.

Supposedly the person who builds something as mundane as a 'better mousetrap' will be 'set for life.' So, keep your mind mulling on the everyday wants and needs in your direct circle of influence. You can save the world later, when you're financially set to do so, right now, let's make ***your*** life better!

Opinions, *(yours or others)* may or may not be worth anything in the end, but what is valuable and powerful is the ideas that they generate!

What am I opinionated about?

For example, John is very opinionated about the multiplication tables and how they are taught to children. He believes this is the crucial time in their lives when children either develop mathematical skills and interests or they don't. This usually decides whether they'll love or hate math for the rest of their lives. He can talk/write about this with a great deal of conviction, citing experiences in his life, in the lives of those close to him and general observations of the world at large.

EJ is very opinionated about the way the credit reporting system works and wants to see responsibility for accurate reporting be mandatory. She also wants to eliminate the use of credit report information used to determine insurance premiums. She feels the "System" is stacked up to make the consumer fail just so that the banks, landlords and insurance companies can charge more and keep most people from ever becoming financially free!

On a grander scale, they are both passionate that alternate energy sources such as wind, solar and hydro need to be commercially developed and available to everyone.

If you don't like the word 'opinionated' because it feels too contrary, exchange it for the word 'passionate.'

What do I know more about than most other people know?

John is truly a master of astronomy. He knows so much about amazing astronomical events. Most of us will be oblivious to these details in our lives, because we just don't know about them. For instance, do you know what an 'Iridium Flare' is? They're really amazing things - and so much fun - and frankly what some UFO reports boil down to. Check out **heavens-above.com** *and learn about them, then check out* **cloudbait.com** *and learn about fireballs. They're both fun websites that people put up dedicated to their favorite subject matter. Pay attention to the ads on the right side of the heavens-above.com home page. This website author has created a web site dedicated to his favorite topic. He provides an amazing amount of free content. He places subtle ads on his site and because of the popularity of this site, these ads create an income stream that pays him for maintaining the website more than if he tried to sell something directly. Keep this example in mind when we talk about using your computer as a resource.*

EJ knows about English Bulldogs. She's been around them all her life. She's bred them and created income streams from two successful litters she raised. She can talk about bulldogs forever, because she even has an amazing "it could only happen to me" story about them that makes for interesting conversation. Easily, she could choose to create an article series about English Bulldogs. There are two passive income streams that this specific knowledge can create: raising animals and writing articles. Stay tuned!

Carrying forward on the alternate energy theme, both EJ and John worked in the Solar Energy generation field and John has worked in the Wind Energy field. So, they both can carry on an informed conversation about alternate energy in general and solar and wind in particular.

What do I *know* that 'they' need to *know*?

One of EJ's authors is a certified nutritionist with very strong, informed opinions about what is in our food!

Her take on Aspartame Toxicity is something everyone should read. The side effects of this food additive is more chilling than most illegal drugs, yet most of us consume it freely!

Creating an Aspartame awareness, to this author, is absolutely critical to the future well being of ourselves and our children!

She wrote a book about this and other valuable information and routinely receives a royalty check. The book also boosts her credibility with her clients, supporting her active income stream. She could easily move to the speaking circuit and probably make even more money than as a practicing nutritionist just telling her story and the story of the people she's helped. Her book could easily be used as a text for a class.*

For Sharon Price, a passionate, informed opinion about the effects of Aspartame has given her the potential for at least a half dozen revenue streams!

* Health and the Domino Effect **ISBN: 1932344551** Sharon Price, CN

What can I passionately talk a long time about and stay interesting to others *(and stay interesting to myself)*?

EJ teaches a 3-hour long class on publishing once a month at the Colorado Free University in Denver, Colorado. She packs a lot in that period of time, and they still usually want to learn more. She sells her book, "The Basics of Profitable Publishing," as the textbook and then sells all her other books, including this one and her fiction novel "Angel On Board," after the class. *

She's created many income streams (both active and passive); tuition, book sales, referrals and she's gained new clients all within the same 3 hours. Last month, this netted her about $350. Now that's not enough to live on, but it also was only 3 hours, plus travel time out of her schedule. When was the last time someone gave you a $350/month raise? We hope we just did!

EJ also talks about "Angel On Board" and her experiences before, during and after writing the book. She talks about her inspiration and what her reader's have told her about how the book affected them. She gets invited to speak at luncheons, civic clubs, radio shows and the like, because she wrote a book and likes to talk about it! All of this eventually leads back to immediate book sales and passive income through Internet book sales later.

*** FreeU.com**

Look in any Community Ed catalog and check out what is being taught - it will range from the usual to the amazing. EJ's favorite recent class was "The Firewalk." We bet there is something that you could teach in this venue. Look at the ideas you write down and see if you could teach a class! You don't have to be a complete expert in the topic, you just have to be motivated to speak about it with accuracy and enthusiasm and know more than most of the other people also interested in this topic.

Our good friend Othniel Seiden, MD teaches "Sex in the Golden Years" and sells that book as the text for that class, but all the rest of his many books are available after class has finished. All topics are fair game!*

*** BoomerBookSeries.com**

What do I want to see changed in the world?

John has a very exciting, workable plan for easing the effects of global warming without disastrous environmental repercussions. As a civilian, he doesn't have the ear of any one who could help him advance this idea. He does have his computer and he writes articles explaining his proposal. Eventually these articles will lead to something (like someone with access). Until then, he gets the freelance income because the subject is timely, affects everyone and is interesting material. This project is in the very beginning stages, but we're sure it'll be very big someday soon!

Perhaps your topic might be something less global, possibly environmental, maybe local. What about your neighborhood? Would you like to see it run differently by the homeowner's association? You don't have to take on your homeowner's association directly, you can approach creating change in many different ways. Maybe you'll even be able to help someone else in another neighborhood who has a similar problem.

The first time someone tells you that your work inspired or helped them will be a moment you'll remember forever and it will inspire you to keep going.

The ideas that thrive and survive even when the going gets tough or the going gets long, are the ideas where there is a purpose or a passion driving them. These are truly world-changing ideas - even if it is just one other person's world - it is worth it!

Do I have an amazing idea?

John speaks frequently about driving through the back roads of Wyoming many years ago. He noticed a small run-down town. About five years later, he drove by the same town and it had changed. It looked alive and thriving. There were signs everywhere about the upcoming Chili Cookoff.

Someone had created an event and deemed their home town the place for it. They must've known how to get publicity, because it seems that the event was successful enough to became a catalyst for the rest of the town to economically recover.

They say that, "Ideas are God's gold coins." This is certainly a case where it was, not just for the originator, but for all the people in their circle of influence!

Now ask yourself: Is there someone I know who is also very opinionated and do I agree with their opinions enough to collaborate on a book or article series or seminar with them?

List these people on a separate page - and go back to this list after you've finished reading this book. If you haven't figured out a path to financial freedom with the tools you have at hand, take heart - and check into the potential of the people you know.

Many books are being created these days based around a theme and contributed to by several authors.

Many people like to see their stories in print - and with the publishing industry and its many options, there are so many ways to produce this type of work and collect the royalties from a book that other people wrote, that you merely compiled.

Whether you collaborate with someone or collect many other people's stories, there's passive income in this for you.

The Value of A Problem

Do you have a problem?
Do you know its solution?

Whether you answered the second question yes or no, the explanation, breakdown, analysis and/or study of the problem is prime fuel for creating products, especially lucrative products.

If you create a product and go to a marketing expert, the first question they will ask you is, "What problem does it solve?" Your answer to that question will determine whether or not they think you have a marketable product.

We're not asking you to dwell on the negative side of your life right now, but do you have a problem, issue, or situation in your life that you would like to see changed *(aside from the fact that you're not financially free yet)*? If so, it is possibly the greatest thing in your life, because it could be the catalyst to your financial freedom.

Write freely and openly. Dig deep as you think about your problem. Identify your problem, who shares your problem and what you'd like to see done about it!

John saw a problem: Many bicycles ride in traffic (either alongside cars or alongside other bicycles) and if the bicycle slows down, there is no way to signal the people behind of the deceleration (or braking). So, he went to find a bike brake light. He found a few on the market, but they required extensive wiring into the bike's frame and braking system, effectively altering the bike's brakes and since he wasn't a bicycle maintenance expert, he wasn't comfortable tampering with his own bike's brakes.

So, what was needed was a bicycle brake light that could just be mounted on the bicycle without altering anything else on the bicycle. He thought about it and LucidBrakes were invented.

You can see the result in a 30 second video clip at LucidBrake.com.

This is a classic example of seeing a problem and fixing it.

Now John makes income on his inventions through selling the product and royalties for the licensing of the product to other companies who manufacture bicycles.

What problem(s) do you have?

How about a sick pet? Have you ever had a sick pet? Almost anyone whose ever owned a pet has received difficult news about them. John and EJ have a business associate who created a website to focus on Pet Health issues, specifically, ***"Alternative Health Care Options for Pets?"******

She got the idea when she learned her elder dog had diabetes. She learned in pretty short order that a multitude of dogs with injuries and illnesses have benefited from acupuncture, massage and reiki. After doing some due-diligence to find out what that really meant to her and her dog, she realized that there wasn't much information available. Surprised by the diagnosis, the number of other people who have pets with diabetes, the lack of information on the topic, and the available treatments, she decided to collect and publish her own information on this and other relevant pet health topics. PetHealthFocus.com is informative and full of options for you and your ailing pet. Again, this is a website packed with content and fueled by subtle ads and affiliate opportunities making it quite lucrative.

Don't underestimate the power of a problem to be a blessing in disguise. Our associate wouldn't have wished diabetes on her pup just so she could have a lucrative business, but when things happen to you - the potential to turn them into good things is always available!

* PetHealthFocus.com

Developing this website helped her deal with her dog's problem as she researched about canine diabetes. Now it is helping many other people do the same research and find relevant information much more quickly.

Let your experiences work to your benefit. People tend to say, "Things always happen for a reason." We'd like to change that slightly and say **"Things always happen for a *GOOD* reason."**

Don't just think about *your* problems, others close to you might be suffering their own problems. Maybe you can see a purpose or silver lining even if they can't.

Maybe you've overcome some problem in your life and want to reach back and help the people who are still suffering with it. Many of the biographies that EJ publishes are just that, very specific events in one person's life overcoming a major obstacle, written with the objective of helping others overcome the same obstacle.

*"What Will Set You Free" is an award-winning biography written by Cynthia James. She overcame a brutally violent childhood. She now speaks about what epiphanies empowered her to be able to release the pain that she carried as baggage into her adult relationships, jobs and daily life. Cynthia created a system that anyone carrying similar baggage can follow and set themselves free from it.**

* What Will Set You Free ISBN: 0-9774761-8-9 Cynthia James

Problems, especially ones you are able to solve, can turn into crusades or drive you to a greater purpose. These are opportunities.

EJ's own first book, "Angel On Board," indeed was about what others would call a problem. It is written about a turbulent time in her life, one that no one would wish upon another human being, but EJ was steadfast through it, knowing it would someday bring her greater good. She didn't have any idea that those experiences would turn into a book, let alone ever help anyone else, yet that is the way it turned out. In retrospect, she wouldn't have changed a thing.

What do you have in your past or present that can be a gift to the world at large? Everyone is here for a Good Reason! Could some experience in your life be the avenue to discover your reason or purpose or calling?

It is truly a wonderful feeling to know that when you do something you feel passionate about, the opportunity for income from it is possible. **We guess that's where the saying comes from, "Do what you love and the money will follow."**

THE VALUE OF EXPERIENCE

Have you ever lived someplace truly unique?

We know people who live (or have lived) in castles, on cruise ships, in haunted houses and in the back woods. Where have you lived that is unusual? Would it make a good story? Would some of the experiences you had there make a good story? Could you collect similar stories from people who've lived similar places?

In the 60's, John's family moved into a big house in the country that had dozens of telephone leads in the basement. Supposedly, the large house had served as a mid-west center for bookies of some sort. With a little research, imagine the stories that could be created from this raw material; a documentary about early 20th century bookies, a historical fiction novel, a biography of the previous owner of the house or the first story in a compilation book about people who moved into the houses of gangsters and what they discovered. The possibilities are endless!

Have you ever lived with someone quite extraordinary?

*Brother Asaiah Bates left his mark on the Alaska hamlet of Homer so deeply there is even an "Asaiah" Day on February 14th. His impact was profound on many people and Martha Ellen Anderson was charged by the late Brother Asaiah to tell his story.**

*Brother Asaiah, **0-9779960-4-2** Martha Ellen Anderson

Do you have an interesting job?

Not everyone has an interesting job, but it is potentially interesting to other people, especially in the same line of work. Did you ever have a strange job in your past? Have you ever had a job that some people would consider a fantasy job (i.e. Forest Ranger, Wine Taster, Caretaker of a Haunted Castle)?

All of these experiences are material for articles in trade journals, magazines, websites or they could be the start of a compilation of stories (yours and others) into a book.

Do you have an idea for a book?

In days past, the only way to find out if a book's idea had any merit was to write a query letter to a publisher and wait to see if they asked you to write the book. With the advent of the Internet, a saavy author can test the market viability of a book using associative marketing techniques.*

Imagine the bookstore book shelf where this future book would be placed and observe the books around it. Set up an amazon.com affiliate account** and create a web page dedicated to these books and your opinion of them. If you're writing a book in a given topic area, there is a reason - these other books inspired you, or they only addressed a portion of what your new book will address... Tell your web visitors what is good about each of these books and then introduce your book idea to them, asking them to leave their e-mail address so that they can be notified when your book is out.

This technique accomplishes many things. First, it establishes a web presence for your future book, next it creates passive income through affiliate sales for you, and third, it creates an 'interested parties' list for you that you can sell to a publisher, another author, or use if you really do write that book.

*Advanced Book Marketing by EJ Thornton

** As long as it is still possible to do that in your state (Colorado no longer has Amazon.com affiliates).

The authors use this system to pre-promote every book idea they have. They call it the "FORESITE" system. It weeds out the bad book ideas, and truly highlights the books that have a great demand. But either way, this method creates passive income through affiliate sales of the books that are already published in the same topic.*

As soon as EJ starts to work on a book to publish, whether it is hers or not, she sets up a FORESITE page. These webpages are also quite valuable to those authors she meets and counsels who never really get around to writing their book. These authors still can benefit from the idea of the book, even if they never accomplish the task of writing it.

It has been an unfortunate observation by EJ (who has taught thousands of authors over the years) that many people who want to write books, never actually do. However, if they set up a FORESITE website, they can still at a minimum create an income stream from their idea.

The more positive side of that observation is, once they actually see there is a demand for the book, they are re-energized and work to actually create the book. The ones who don't see too much income from the FORESITE based on their future book are grateful that they didn't waste their time writing something that didn't have a market.

http://writerssummit.com/foresite.php

Practical Application

Now, as you read the next section of the book, keep the ideas you jotted down in the forefront of your mind. If new ideas are sparked by the content in this next section, stop, write them down and then resume reading.

The "gold" is in the ideas. You'll never be able to do them all, but we bet you'll end up being surprised at which idea really brings in the big bucks. They all matter - stay inspired - it's fun!

The content that follows is designed to give you a way to turn those ideas into something that creates income.

We have created a pretty hefty list of ideas in the following sections. We don't expect that you'll be enthused about all of them, in fact some may be a downright turn off at first, but read it with financial freedom in mind and see if your perspective changes - it just might. If it does, great, if not - just read on! We're sure something will click.

This is not a comprehensive list, we couldn't possibly know all there is to know about potential passive income streams because frankly many are being invented at this moment! So, if you can create your own style of developing passive income... ***Fantastic!***

How To Get Paid For What You Already Know

Freelancing

Writing articles is a very lucrative side business. With the advent of the Internet, everyone is searching for 'content.' Everyone wants 'content' for their magazines, newsletters, websites, etc. You can create a very nice side income by writing articles. Once you've created an article, you've created content! You've created a product!

What can you write about? You just listed a ton of ideas in the Idea Fest portion. Any one of those could be an amazing article series that you could sell either to online e-zines or real world glossy paper magazines. Note that if you don't sell your creative rights, you can sell the same content over and over again.

When you sell your creative rights (also known as ***exclusive*** *print rights), your ability to make money with that article is done.*

*However, when you sell '**first** print rights,' you get paid only once, but you reserve your ability to make money off the article again by selling 'secondary serial rights.' This allows you to sell the same content as many times as you want to.*

Freelancing passes most of the passive income tests. You do the major portion of the work once and get paid for it over and over again. It is not time dependent. However, it doesn't create money if you don't re-sell it, so you can't walk away from it.

After you write an article once, you can tweak it for a different audience, saying virtually the same thing using a slightly different angle, and voila, a new product that you can again sell 'first print rights' for. You've created yet another product!

There are websites that pay writers for original articles. The pay starts out low, but it gets better and better the more that you contribute. There is no limit to how much you contribute, however they pay the most for exclusive rights to the work. This limits how much you can make on each work, but there is no limit to how much you submit each month, so if you happen to have a stash of writings, you can get a lot of money quickly, by submitting it to these websites. We will put a list of the most current article submission websites on our own webpage:*

*WritersSummit.com/Articles.php

The players can change frequently, so instead of publishing this information where it will become outdated, we'll keep the website up to date. If you'd like to follow up on this income stream, check out our page for the latest resources.

One of our authors, Othniel Seiden has written an article that he is so passionate about that he includes it each one of his non-fiction health books. It is about quitting smoking. His advice is to keep your creative rights so that you can use the same content again and again in different books. His various books are about age, weight and sex, yet he uses the same chapter in each, because it is applicable in each. Once you have something good, if you keep the creative rights, you can use it over and over again!

EJ counsels many of her book authors to start with article writing. They think that the only way to get their message out is to write a book, but they don't have all their content fleshed out yet (or they don't feel they have 'enough'), therefore their idea sits on the shelf, potentially becoming obsolete information.

* Sex in the Golden Years **ISBN: 0-9801941-0-5** Othniel J. Seiden, MD & Jane Bilett, Ph.D.
* The Second Half Begins at 50 **ISBN: 0-9801941-1-3** Othniel J. Seiden, MD & Jane Bilett, Ph.D.
* Heavy & Healthy **ISBN: 0-9779960-5-0** Othniel J. Seiden, MD & Jane Bilett, Ph.D.

All of Otti's books can be found at BoomerBookSeries.com

What she's told them to do is to start publishing the articles in trade journals *(topic oriented magazines)*, and to keep writing more in the article series. Somehow, writing a series of articles doesn't sound as daunting as writing a book. They feel they can get their heads around the project, actually do it (big step) and get published and get paid. They get their message out - which is all they really wanted to do in the first place - and it makes them money!

Article writing can start out quite lucratively. When you finally have enough articles to compile into a non-fiction book on the topic, the name recognition you've created and the following you have will already have established you. It will help you market the book. Your previously published works improve your chance for a publishing advance and better royalties.

WRITING BOOKS

Now that you're published...

Doesn't that sound nice? It's well within your grasp. So, now that you're published, what do you do next?

The easiest thing might be to keep writing. If you keep writing a series of articles on the same topic, you have rich material for a book.

Books can be quite frustrating or quite lucrative depending on how you approach the project. There are ways to get published for free and get your books out.

Many authors, especially first-time authors, make the mistake of assuming the goal when you have written a book is to get it published.

The goal is not to be published, but to be read!

Getting published is fairly easy these days with the advent of the digital press. So getting the work produced is no longer the problem. But the age-old issue remains to be overcome and that issue is marketing the book and getting it in the hands of the readers.

Publish your book with a plan for its release, growth and transformation into other things, such as speaking engagements, future books and other forms of passive income that are just too numerous to mention here.

EJ and many other people have written about this. If you choose to go this way, before you spend a dime printing your book, please read at least three books on publishing. There are so many ways to approach a publishing project and one will work for you. Figure out if it is self-publishing, commercial publishing, partner publishing or some interesting combination of the three!

There will always be updated information on this topic, so we promise to keep this webpage* current with the latest and greatest the industry has to offer!

* EJThornton.com
* WritersSummit.com
* ThorntonPublishing.com

WRITING E-BOOKS

The e-publishing devices such as Amazon.com's Kindle and Barnes & Noble's Nook have taken the reading public by storm. Sophisticated cell phones have e-pub readers built right into them. Accessing these e-publishing tools is easier than in years past as well.

As of Christmas 2009, Amazon.com reported they sold more Kindle versions of books than they did of physical books.

Kindle makes it very easy to publish using their format. Once you have a set of articles, it is really simple to sign on to Amazon.com and go to the Kindle section of the website, create an account and publish content. There are no other publishers, there are no ISBN's or bar codes necesssary, only content.

Having a good cover helps sell Kindle books, so if you're going to publish in this venue, please only publish edited content and create a pleasant workable book cover.

Once you have published a Kindle product, all the power of the Amazon.com sales engine is available to you. Their commission is high. However, there are no expenses to get your book listed in Kindle, so all the income received from it is purely profit. Since it does not involve creating a product or shipping a product or order processing at all, Kindle is a true form of passive income.

All of EJ's books are potential to become Kindle books - Angel On Board, Advanced Book Marketing, this book. In fact, just as an experiment, EJ published a book only to Kindle - with an abbreviated version of this content just to see if it was worthwhile to do. It only had about 25 pages of content and she sold it for $2.99 - of which she receives $1.05. This book sells consistently and adds to the passive income streams of the authors.

Barnes & Noble's Nook is harder to get published under. However, they are working to create more functionality than Amazon's Kindle, so watching the e-book readers develop is interesting.

So much free software exists that this avenue to create passive income is available to all. Sigil is a free software package to create e-books in the e-Pub format. PrimoPDF creates PDF's for free. ClickBank.com will take a PDF product into their inventory. So, the same content published in Kindle can be quickly turned around and published either in Sigil or PrimoPDF and placed into the ClickBank system to create an additional passive income stream quickly and effectively.

Although things are changing rapidly in this arena, e-Pub readers are readily available on most cell phones. So, creating small cell phone apps is available to the technically saavy among you as well.

Instant fulfillment of electronic products through online merchants already set up for these transactions creates the potential for everyone to create passive income streams for multiple products.

Promotion of these digital products is of course the trick. However, when partnering with powerhouses like ClickBank and their band of affiliates and Amazon.com or Barnes & Noble, most of the work is done if you just take advantage of the tools they provide. Then of course, you have to supplement with an online presence other places like in Twitter or Facebook or whatever the next great social media site turns out to be.

TEACHING

At first glance, teaching doesn't pass any of the tests of passive income. It is time dependent - you have to tell people where and when you teach. You can't walk away - you're the teacher! You can not make money if you're not there.

However, teaching is a way to amplify your hourly wage and create secondary income streams (both passive and active). Read on!

Usually when you teach (unless you're a private tutor), you have several students in a class. It takes you just as much time to lecture to 10 students as it does to teach 1. But if they've paid the tuition, then you have 10 times the money for the same amount of time. Now consider that if you can teach 10 students, you can probably teach 50 or 100 or even more. Your time involvement is identical, but the proceeds are proportionally greater!

Teaching usually has other perks. If you're a good teacher, most students want to learn more from you. So, if you have more than one subject you teach - you can probably sell them another class - or your book about the subject, or some other service that will enhance their learning.

If you want to go the teaching route, be sure and create class materials that you sell to the students in addition to the tuition. Create basic course materials, then add on a set for 'continuing education' and sell those after class is done. Sell whatever else you have available at the back of the room - other books, services, other classes or even other people's stuff (arrange a commission agreement with them as long as their products validate what you teach).*

Get your student's names and contact information for your next class and ask them to refer you to someone they know - *referral marketing is amazing.*

* Other people often have products and services they want promoted. Referral and commission income from their products is true passive income.

How To Get Paid For What You Want To Learn

Research can be lucrative.

Have you always wanted to know more about a certain place? Do you wish you could take up an expensive hobby? Maybe you feel like you can't afford to go there or do that because of lack of money. Turn that around. Immerse yourself in the topic and find out all there is to know about it. Then start writing about it or figure out some other way to provide more information on the topic, i.e. through affiliate links or writing web articles or creating an online community like PetHealthFocus.com.

If you are to believe the financial guru's who espouse "The Power of Attraction" - you'll find out you're visiting that exotic place or taking up that hobby quicker than you ever imagined. If you make a vow to pay for it only with the passive income you create from it, then it won't cost you a thing! And it will probably be tax deductible! *Bonus!!!*

PetHealthFocus.com again, is a very good example of how this works. Our business associate wasn't versed in dog health issues, she just was suddenly faced with them. When she couldn't find what she wanted, she researched the subject as thoroughly as she could and created an online business. She is technically savvy and was able to create a website by herself, so she had a head start. But you can do the same with all the free (and low fee) tools* that exist on the web. Even if you don't feel technically strong, if you can browse the Internet, and write a word document, you are most of the way there. Later, when we speak of affiliate programs, we will give you step by step instructions for creating your own website or getting the help you need to get this done.

Even if it does feel like a daunting task, the Internet and creating a website which creates income for you is by far the cheapest and easiest method to start receiving immediate passive income. It is a skill worth learning!

We're sure that you've heard the phrase, "Stop working for your money, make your money work for you!" That is one way to look at passive income. But what else, in addition to money can you get to work for you?

We bet you already have resources that can turn into revenue streams. You don't have to spend a dime to acquire new things. You will have to work to set up the system to get these resources to start generating income, but the raw resource is already yours! Let's explore some of the ways your resources can turn into your work horses.

You probably also have stuff not on this list, look around you and see what might just be untapped gold right there in your living room or garage.

Stay open to the inspiration!

Make Your Resources Work For You

COMPUTERS

With the advent of the Internet, everyone's computer is a potential cash machine. We're sure you've heard of "webeneurs" and every other aspect of people who've made it big using their computer to do something new.

Not too many of us can get by without their computer - at least not for very long!

There are good ways and bad ways to try to earn money using your computer. We will not address e-mail marketing campaigns at all. We get tired of e-mail solicitations, so we refuse to teach it.

However, there are many other terrific ways to make money using your computer.

If you're technically savvy or a computer programmer by trade, stay keenly aware of any thought process that starts with the words, "They should make a program that does..." If you've identified a problem that can be solved by a computer program - write it!

If you're not a programmer, there are ways for you to contract to have a program created. For example, you can use the freelance networking site **e-lance.com.** Once you've paid for a program's development and as long as you signed a **work-for-hire*** agreement with the developer, you own the rights and can resell the commodity. This approach might be a long-shot for you non-programmers out there, but the potential for it still exists - very much so. Just get the bids and do a cost benefit analysis. Selling digital products is very lucrative if you set it up properly.

*Examples of such a program are mortgage interest calculations, mortgage payoff calculations, credit card payoff calculations, astronomical calculations, mileage calculations and passive income calculations.** Many more of these home-grown programs that have worked their way up into full-fledged products include all the accounting applications, inventory and order fulfillment workflows.*

If there is a problem to be solved, solve it! Even if you're not a programmer you can find a way to get it done!

* The phrase "work for hire" must be in the contract between you and any developer of an intellectual property if you want to own the rights to be able to resell it. If you do not use those words, they will still own the creative rights. To find out more about intellectual property go to the website:

http://WritersSummit.com/IntellectualProperty.php

Creating your own website to sell your products digitally is an amazing way to create a money machine. E-books, photographs, comic books, films have all proven to be great avenues for passive income. Predict and capitalize now on whatever the next-greatest medium turns out to be. If it can be sold digitally, it is a potential passive income stream.

Using the website **ClickBank.com**, you can sell most any digital product that you want to. You don't even have to have your own website *(although it is highly recommended)*. You can record yourself giving a speech, put the file on your computer, upload it to clickbank.com *(after you've created an account)* and get paid for any that sell. If you allow it to go into the affiliate program, then you have a multitude of sales reps putting it on their web pages to sell it for you! It is amazing how fast you can get digital products to market and how well some of these websites get it out there with *(and for)* you.

John created a website called sun-track.com where he can espouse all of his solar energy knowledge and sell many solar energy related products on a monetized review website. This website sells digital products off of the ***clickbank.com*** *website. When John has some solar energy products (not just articles) that he wants to sell in digital form, this website is the platform that he will launch them from. Until then, he just receives generous commisions from the products he's already endorsing there. Note: He did his due diligence and researched these products for validity of concept, value of information and reputability of the vendor selling. If you want to make a name for yourself in the industry, you need to research carefully who you partner with.*

Although most of these digital partners will show you how fast you can get your digital product up and available for sale, if you rely on their efforts without putting any effort in yourself, you will end up being frustrated and greatly disillusioned by this whole exercise. Their sales copy makes it look easy and seem effortless. It is easy - but it is not completely done for you. The main problem is that most people "don't know what they don't know," and they often learn a very painful lesson about relying on another person's efforts. Applying effort towards your own dreams is what pays off best.

Internet

Affiliate Programs

Affiliate programs are the crown jewel of the Internet where passive income is concerned. This is the way for any Internet marketer to turn you into their sales rep. They pay generous commissions and all you have to do is put special code on your website *(or in your e-mail signature)* to sell their stuff.

Almost everyone has ads on their websites - from the major players to the 'mom and pops.' If you go to **CNN.com**, you'll see google ads there. If you go to **HeavensAbove.com** - you'll see google ads there. If you go to **Sports-Top-10.com** - you'll see google ads there, as well as others.

The main problem with affiliate sales on the net is that most web masters aren't methodical or deliberate about it. If they find an affiliate program they like, they slap the banner ad on their 'affiliate' page in between two other banner ads that may or may not be related to what the site is about. These ads are seldom noticed, and these ads will likely not produce much passive income. Many people 'don't believe' in affiliate programs because they don't work for them. It is understandable. Most people who run their own websites and put this type of page up, don't understand search engine optimization or Internet marketing. They have a golden opportunity, but it gets lost in the noise of 'the net.'

The way to approach these affiliate opportunities is to do so very deliberately. Find a product that you like, get the banner ad from it and build a page around it. **The only thing that gets the attention of the search engines is textual content - *not graphics.***

So, put text content **around the banner ad**, because no matter how spiffy the ad might be, it won't be seen by the search engine spiders who grade the webpage by how relevant it may be to any given search.

What content do you put on your web page? First, you look to see what sales copy the advertised product's website has on its page. You find out what problems it solves. For instance, **StickySheets.com** is a pet hair cleanup product. If you have a web site that has anything to do with animals or cleaning, you need to become an affiliate of StickySheets.

Type in StikySheets.com (without the 'c'), wait for the redirect to the home page, dig around and learn about the product and when you are ready to sign up as an affiliate, go to the following page by typing the address in the browser *(you won't find a link to click on):*
http://stickysheets.com/Affiliate_Program.php

StickySheets, like most affiliate programs on the web, provides you with tools to help you help them sell their stuff. The common misconception, however, is that these tools are sufficient to create the income stream, when in reality, they are not. They are only the necessary first part. The StickySheet's website is filled with wonderful information, testimonials, other uses, frequently asked questions and a huge amount of sales copy content that can be used as material for you to help sell the product on your website.

PetHealthFocus.com is also a StickySheets affiliate. Their site is designed to help pet owners deal with pet health problems. They've chosen to highlight a product which cleans up after pets (StickySheets). In this case, the text content of the pet information already on the website also puts StickySheets' information in front of the visitor. It is a win/win system.

Yet a better way to do this, is to create a page based on the product you want to sell and incorporate that page into the rest of your site. Ask yourself (or glean it from the parent website), "If I didn't know the name of this product or its manufacturer, what websearch would I use to try and find it?" *For example, Angel on Board is an "Angel Book." StickySheets "cleans up pet hair."* Then write a two to five sentence paragraph around that subject, in your own words (but use the specific search terms in your text). Make only claims that the parent company has also claimed or that you personally have experienced. *You will get banned from affiliate programs if you create false claims around a product.* You can take tidbits from their testimonials or frequently asked questions and use them as a source to create your paragraph. Once the paragraph has been created, and the banner ad code is in place, create a page that is named for the search topic, *(not the product).* For example, use a web page name of 'PetHairCleanup.htm' or 'AngelBook.htm' - instead of naming it for the product. *Don't worry if the name is too long, the point of this page is to be found by search engines, so no one should ever have to type it in.*

The text on your web page between the **< title > < /title >** brackets also should reflect the search term and the product. For example, use the verbiage, **Pet Hair Cleanup Product - StickySheets.** Or **Great New Angel Book called Angel On Board.** If you use a software product to create web pages, this will simply be called the Title area. It will show in the very top caption in the border of the displayed webpage. Most every software package allows you to view the code it creates, to make sure what you are putting there is correct. Even if you don't read html code very well, just look for the bookends < title > < /title >.

There are at least 7 more tips for creating web pages that show well in search engines that we use all the time. If you want to know more, go to **http://writerssummit.com/WebOptimization.php.** There are tips and tricks on this page, as well as books for sale through EJ's amazon.com affiliate website.

It isn't a matter of how many products you sell like this, it is a matter of how well they sell. So, give each product you choose to represent about an hour's worth of research - and you will reap great rewards.

If you can group several similar products on one page, that is terrific. Be sure these product are relevant to the search terms however. *You will lose traffic and can get black-listed if it is perceived that you brought a visitor in on a false pretense.* So, just play straight and create a win/win and it will work out really well.

As in the above example on Web Optimization, we found twelve books on amazon.com that fit the Web Optimization category, developed content around Web Optimization and that page now brings in visitors looking to find information on Web Optimization.

This single page provides us with at least three different ways to make passive income from a visit, but first the visitor gets the information they came to find. We might get a commission if they buy one of the books from amazon.com, they might decide to consult with us or buy a product we sell directly, or if they click out through a relevant google ad/search, we still get paid. It is a win/win/win.

Every page on your site should have a search within the site, and a search the web option that are provided for you through an affiliate program. All the major search engines provide their own affiliate programs that furnish this option. Many times you need to apply and wait for approval because they want to be sure your site's content is appropriate, but most every site with usable, 'non-porn' content can get approved.

Affiliate programs like amazon.com are product oriented. They sell so many products that you are sure to find something that is complimentary *(not competitive)* with your webpage. Create new *(or get additional)* income by adding these products as options to your web pages. So even if the visitor don't buy *your* book, you can still make a buck on someone else's book. It's okay, the numbers eventually add up to financial freedom.

There are also "super-affiliate" programs like:
commissionjunction.com or **asseenontv.com**

These sites make agreements with product manufacturers to run their affiliate programs, saving the manufacturers the headache of sending out commission checks. These sites also train up their affiliates in site optimization and other pertinent web topics. It is in their best interest to help you do well, so they work hard at training the new super-affiliate.

If the affiliate just creates a "banner farm" on their website, it won't do well. So, these super-affiliate sites allow you to use their sales copy and give you other tips to make it as easy as possible to be successful.

Many of these sites train their affiliates on topics such as proper/effective ad placement on a webpage. They teach valuable web skills gleaned from practical application. It is a free education, all the better that it might be lucrative. They provide the information free, again, because they win when you win. They get their cut, when you do.

Almost every product sold on the Internet is in one of these affiliate programs. Maybe the product is like StickySheets and manages their own affiliate program. Maybe they hired a company to manage their affiliate program. Maybe they sell through amazon.com (which also feeds borders.com and target.com - which also have their own affiliate programs).

Our advice is, if you're just starting out,

1. Figure out what your topic of interest is.

2. Decide what products you want to produce if any to service that topic *(i.e. book, class, articles, etc)*. Get working on them (go through your Idea Fest notebook).

3. Register and get a domain name hosted We use **GoDaddy.com** as our domain registrar.

4. Find a few products on the Internet which also address the topic. Sign up for their affiliate programs. Set up web pages for these products on your website.

This does two things - one, it starts pulling in affiliate income right away, two, it establishes your website as relevant for this subject matter even before you have your own product ready (if you ever do). Three, it gives you an amazing head start if indeed you do decide to write a book, an e-book, or sell a digital recording of a class, etc.

5. Release your product(s) on to the website.

6. Promote the product via the website and via other tools you learned about here or through your research.

7. Assess your success *(usually quarterly)*. If it was successful - repeat it as many times as you need to create a passive income stream that exceeds your expenses.

Assessing quarterly helps, because very few people are 'overnight successes' on the Internet. It takes time for the search engines to find your site, among other reasons. So, get it set up, then relax and assess it periodically. Keep good records and determine if your site is a winning or a losing proposition. If it isn't bringing in money or bringing in as much as you thought, take time to assess why, make adjustments and keep trying. The magic formula will reveal itself. Keep learning from the people who are successful at this and learn from what they do. If they can do it, so can you!

Many programs teach how to build a website, but the most comprehensive approach we've experienced is called **Affiloblueprint.** This is a 12-week course that teaches you how to find something that sells well through websites, and how to create a website around it. This program provides tools, tips and tricks to create a review website and is well worth the investment, if this is one of the ways you choose to create your passive income.

Stuff

Auction Sites

No doubt you've also heard "E-bay" success stories, where people go out and collect items they think they can sell on e-bay. They take a picture, do a little data entry, sit back and collect income from their auctioned items. Of course, they have to ship those items, so there it is not a completely passive stream of income, and you can't walk away from this and still collect money, but it can work in a multiplicative way and make the time you spend in it very lucrative.

Some businesses have popped up that sell your things through these auction sites for you. That is truer passive income, because all you need to do is drop the stuff off, then pick up the check. It is not time dependent and you aren't doing the actual work.

Whether you sell items yourself or hire it out, this is a good way to create more income. If you like to hit garage sales, produce your own products or are a recovering pack rat, this might be a perfect opportunity for you.

Used Books

Another great feature of Amazon.com is that they allow people to resell their used books on their site. It is quite simple to click on the button "Sell Yours Here" and list the books you may have stored on the bookshelves of your basement, garage or attic.

One of EJ's authors did not have enough cash in hand to start the publishing process, let alone pay for a website or an editor or a graphic designer. However, she had collected many books over the years and started to sell these. She ended up financing her whole book project using her used book inventory.

EJ and John always look for books that are going stale on the bookstore shelves (discounted more than 75% of the original price) and buy them and list them on Amazon.com for at least 3 times what they bought them for.

Is this passive income? It certainly creates an income stream that wasn't present prior. However, it does require listing of the books on the Amazon.com or E-bay websites and shipping them when they sell. It isn't much work for a minimum 3-fold return on an investment. Passive Income, kinda... Good idea, definitely.

TELEPHONES

FREE TELECONFERENCE SITES

If you decide that you'd rather not 'write a book,' but instead speak about a topic because it is easier for you to speak than to write, then find out more about the free teleconference services on the web.*

There are many of these services and they enable you to create a platform where you're the speaker and you have people dial into the teleconference or tele-seminar and listen to you teach.

These sites make money on their additional and optional services and the long distance charges, as well as ads they place, etc. So their service to you is virtually free. Many of these provide a free (or low fee) recording service. So, after you're done speaking, you can keep the recording and do with it what you please (such as sell it as a digital product on clickbank.com or off of your website).

Listen to a sample class on the four types of publishing at **http://EJThornton.com.**

*http://FreeConferenceCalling.com

The other thing that you can do is to transcribe this information and create multiple articles, or start forming chapters of your next book with the material, and start the passive income strategies that way.

EJ, John and many of EJ's authors and acquaintances have used this technique to kick start gathering content for a non-fiction book or article series. For example, this book takes some of its information from a 4-week long telecourse that EJ put together called "Seven Ways to Make Every Day a Payday." (This telecourse is available for sale if you want a way to gather up more ideas to create passive income.) During the taping of these telephone calls, the interviewer, Roger House put into practice many of the techniques from the telecourse and he started making passive income, even as he was taking the course. These ideas work, if you put them to work!*

*http://ForTheWealthOfAll.com

Other People's Work

Digital reprint rights.

Amazingly enough, there are people on the web who write things and then allow you to sell them for them and let you keep all the money. It's true. They're in it for the name recognition, not the money. They typically sell a much higher priced package of services and use this technique to further their celebrity status. It is a good way to create some passive income without having to create a product yourself.

There are rules to follow - some people allow you to do this for a licensing fee (most are very reasonable). Some allow you to do this for free as long as you include the author's name, e-mail address, etc. Their stipulations for use will be in contract form and you'll have to follow them exactly.

Search for "digital reprint rights," or "free digital reprint rights" on google and see who's doing it now. We learned of this opportunity through webinars and lectures given by the publicity expert Paul Hartunian. If you do a search on his name, it is certain that you will find his information. He also typically uses referrals and affiliate links to others who are offering their reprint rights.

PUBLIC DOMAIN MATERIAL

Copyrights have expiration dates and that date is 70 years after the author dies. So, any published material by an author who has been dead for more than 70 years has passed into the public domain. This means that anyone can reprint this material and it is perfectly legal and above board.

*As an experiment, EJ republished the book "The Science of Getting Rich" on the website http://**ForTheWealthOfAll.com**. Wallace Waddles died in 1911, so as of 1981, his work passed into the public domain. Wallace wrote in the language of his time and it was not gender inclusive, so EJ adapted his words to be gender inclusive and republished them on the website. This was an experiment in passive income. The words of Wallace Waddles are free on the website, but the book is available at Amazon.com and Google adsense links surround the information. This site creates passive income for EJ, but the content is completely Waddles'.*

Referrals

Referral bonuses are an amazing way to create passive income just by talking to people. If someone you know has a great service or product, find out what they are paying for referrals. Many times they belong to a networking club or two and actively ask for referral clients or customers. They will pay a percentage for a lead or a sale. Ask them what it is and how they track it. If this is a person you appreciate, likely you've already been sending them customers that they'd be willing to pay you for.

The typical makeup of a networking club is realtors, chiropractors, dentists, insurance professionals, bankers, massage therapists, accountants, small business owners, financial planners and so on. Visit a group - usually you can do that for the price of a lunch - and pay attention to the people who pay for referrals. The ones who go to these meetings are actively seeking referrals and will usually pay just for the lead! Collect their business cards!

Do you like your dentist? Did you have a good experience with the realtor that sold you your house? Call them up and ask if they pay a referral fee for new clients. Ask them if they belong to a networking club and if you could come visit it to see if it is for you. Go and learn from that experience. Then write down on a separate page in your notebook a list of professions who always need new clients. By those professions, write the names of the people you know who practice that profession. You have a great start at creating a passive income stream, because all you have to do is recommend people you already like to people you also already like. It is a win/win/win situation! Bonus!

EJ runs a publishing company and she pays $50 for every author who signs with her. Usually it is only her other authors who send her referrals, but she is willing to pay this to anyone who successfully sends her an author she ultimately represents. ***Who do you know?****

*E-mail EJ at EJ@EJThornton.com

Wall Space & Floor Space

Advertisers need space and they are getting more and more creative about the places they are putting their ads.

Some people are driving cars with large magnetic billboards on their doors advertising their business or a business they've been paid to advertise. Your car is a potential billboard (therefore a potential passive income generator).

In rural areas - space abounds, fences abound. As long as it doesn't violate some county ordinance, put up a billboard saying 'Advertise here' with your name and number on it. Let them contact you.

Fences inside the city limits are usually zoned more restrictively, but if it is legal for you to do so, create a banner sign. Banner signs are reasonably cheap and easy to create using computer files. Put up a banner on your chain link fence. It'll give you a bit more privacy and it'll make some money.

Who loves this kind of ad?

The same ones who are paying for referrals - realtors especially will advertise anywhere they can. It is in their best interest to create "name branding." So, offer it, if you have the space to rent.

Floor space is another commodity you can use. If you run a business, make sure the floor and wall space is used efficiently by having bulletin boards wherever you can. One of the more brilliant passive income businesses we've seen lately, is billboards on the back of bathroom stalls and above urinals. Granted, we are bombarded with advertisements everywhere - and even the toilet is not sacred enough space. But this is a captive audience and most people read anything they can while they are stuck on the pot! If you know of an establishment where their bathrooms are still pristine (or at least the walls are bare), create this business. You need a little Plexiglass and a couple of screws and two or three good advertisers - voila, you have created passive income!

Gum ball machines and vending machines are a lucrative passive income. These are usually low maintenance devices that sell things while you're not around. You have to keep them stocked, but if it is lucrative enough, you can pay someone else to do that! Some of these machines make really good money. Each of them are owned by someone. And so many different things are being sold through them. Gum ball machine vendors easily found by doing a google search on the Internet.

If we had wanted to create more passive income, we could have struck a deal with one of these businesses and recommended you contact them, giving them a special code for us to get a referral fee, but we want this book to stand on its own merits. If we benefit from any of the businesses we recommend in this book, we will let you know, so that you can process that information in your decision making.

We know these avenues for passive income exist. What we want most for you is to understand how many of them there are and that everyone who wants to, can achieve financial freedom!

Web Page Space

Web advertisers also need space to place their ads. If you do have a website, there are web advertisers willing to pay you to place ads on your website.

The most well-known one of these is Google. Google has the Adsense program, which is the compliment to the Adwords program. Advertisers use the Adwords system to create ads, and Google uses web sites that subscribe to the Adsense system to place those ads. If someone clicks on those ads, then the website owner is paid.

Banner ads still exist, however they are not as favored as they were when this book was first published.

Yahoo has the Kontera system, which creates hyperlinks around the words you already have on the websites.

The point is, advertisers need places to advertise and websites, especially popular websites can create income streams for their owners.

http://kontera.com
http://google.com/adsense

Newsletter Space

Like a website, newsletters give excellent opportunities to sell advertisements and to create a membership base.

Most newsletters come with a subscription fee. If you have a set of articles, publishing these in a newsletter format and selling subscriptions to these newsletters creates passive income potential.

Your membership list is quite lucrative as well, as many advertisers will buy lists. This isn't a popular thing to do with the people who are on your list, however, lists of potential clients are really quite valuable to many businesses. Collecting names can create passive income streams a myriad of ways.

Table Space

We'll just touch on this topic, as it is not truly passive income at all. However, like teaching, it has the potential to amplify time and space into a lucrative experience.

EJ created an event for authors, called The Rocky Mountain Writer's Summit. This event created many types of income streams, some passive, some active. **http://WritersSummit.com** is a the website dedicated to the event, and many of the service providers bought advertising space in its online directory. Corporate sponsors wanted to advertise and associate themselves with the event. So, creating a space at the event to place banners and signs for these advertisers created passive income.

Selling vendor space created passive income by artifically dividing up space into valuable commodities vendors paid good money for. At the event, books, tapes and other products were sold. Attendees signed up for vendor newsletters and to be notified for future product releases. These memberships to newsletters represent streams of passive income for more than just the organizers.

Organizing these events is anything but passive, but when done well, long-term passive income streams can be created that are direct results of the event.

FINGERS

Do you love to create?

Do you knit, sew, needle-point, paint, make stained glass windows, tie flies, work with wood or anything else creative or crafty? Is this what you enjoy doing when you aren't actively working your job? If so, then do it and sell the work.

There are a ton of places to sell your work; trade shows, craft fairs, the Internet, E-bay, garage sales. Take the money you make from this and put it into a savings account and let it earn interest.

Set a goal for the account and when it has reached that goal, shift the money into some other avenue that can create more passive income. The creation of the work isn't passive - so we can't really call this passive income. However, the proceeds for it can be turned into passive income. Also, if you get really good at selling it, teach other people to make it (duplicate yourself), sell their work for them and take a cut. Who knows, you might have just created a new cottage industry doing something you really love.

Just like if you have a strong opinion about something and can write about it, turn your craft, skill or hobby into multiple revenue streams.

If you are a master of your craft, you can teach it to others, multiplying your hourly wage. Other people will pay to learn from someone who can teach them - you'll be surprised how many.

Write articles about your craft. Collect them, create a book and otherwise continue to capitalize on your skill.

Pets

Do you have a pet that you invested in? Do you have a full bred dog, cat, mouse, fish or horse? Can you breed them and sell them? Can you write about your experiences with them?

EJ was raised with English Bulldogs and has a brilliant passion for them. English Bulldog enthusiasts will generally stop everything they're doing and approach any English Bulldog whether or not they know the owner. The owners also know this happens frequently - and everyone seems to belong to a small sub-culture. We're sure that most breed enthusiasts belong to their own sub-culture. So, each niche is well established.

If you can write about the topic, do so. Every breed has a web page, a wikipedia entry, amazon.com products, an E-bay thread and more. So, finding products suited to your specific breed is no problem.

EJ bred three English Bulldog litters. The first one was very successful and yielded five healthy male puppies. The second one had four pups, two male, two female and one of the females died at three days. The third one only yielded one pup, and EJ lost both the pup and the mom during a C-Section to deliver the puppy.

You can see by this that she has experience with dog breeding and English Bulldogs that relatively few people have had; some great results and some very sad results. But the lessons learned along the way and the money earned (especially with the first litter) were quite valuable on several levels.

You have assets everywhere. You just need to know how to look for them. If you buy a purebred pet, breeding them at least once should yield you some income. If you buy a male, then the siring process is pure passive income. The owners usually get paid up-front for the 'use' of their pet or get the proceeds from the 'pick of the litter.' It's a pretty sweet deal if you have a male purebred pet.

Writing about the experience, or any of the other passive income ideas could send that investment of a purebred into the profit column pretty quickly.

EJ had a one-in-a-billion experience when delivering the second litter of puppies. Her daughter and the puppies were born on the same day, only a couple of hours apart. And that was only the beginning of the coincidences on June 12, 1989! She could write a whole book just about the amazing events of that day. If you ever meet her in person, ask - but have an hour to spare!

Make Your Money Work For You!

Once you grasp the concept that tools must work for you to help you create passive income, looking at the most obvious tool - money - is essential.

Earned Interest

When someone defines "Passive Income," earned interest on money deposited at a bank is a classic example. It's an easy way to illustrate how money can earn more money.

This is truly passive income, because it passes the litmus tests for passive income:

1. It is not dependent on your time or effort.
2. You're not materially involved with it (except to actually open the account).
3. You don't have to pay attention to it, yet the interest keeps compounding and your balances keep growing.

This is a very conservative approach to passive income, but it works. If you get a windfall of money, a bank is a good, safe place to keep it. And if you get a significant amount of money, most banks have higher yielding accounts, which make more interest and make more income for the owner. If you have the money, this is one sure fire way to make your money work for you.

There are better, faster and still secure ways of creating passive income, other than "money in the bank" - but this is literally that - "*money in the bank.*" You must be the one to decide if keeping it there will help you meet your passive income goals. Only a truly significant amount of money can do that, but if you have it - you win! You're financially free if you can get your interest income to exceed your personal expenses.

Many stories are told of people receiving some major windfall and then losing it all in just a few months - usually winding up bitter, cynical and worse off than ever financially. To understand why this happens, read "*Secrets of The Millionaire Mind*" by T. Harv Eker and watch for the concept of the 'financial thermostat.'

http://WritersToBelieveIn.com/THarvEker.php

If these people would simply put the money somewhere that would keep earning more money for a few months, they could get used to the idea that they "had money." They could create a reasonable plan for this money to make its own money and pay them forever. They would then have changed their financial thermostats forever, creating their financial freedom.

Calculate how much money you would need to have in the bank at 10% interest to generate enough passive income to match your current annual income.

For example - To make 40,000 a year in passive income using only a savings account that pays 10% interest, you'd have to start with $382,000. Assuming you could leave the money there the whole year to compound the interest, the results would look like this.*

Month	Balance	Interest
January	$382,000.00	$ 3,183.33
February	$385,183.33	$ 3,209.86
March	$388,393.19	$ 3,236.61
April	$391,629.80	$ 3,263.58
May	$394,893.39	$ 3,290.78
June	$398,184.16	$ 3,318.20
July	$401,502.37	$ 3,345.85
August	$404,848.22	$ 3,373.74
September	$408,221.95	$ 3,401.85
October	$411,623.80	$ 3,430.20
November	$415,054.00	$ 3,458.78
December	$418,512.79	$ 3,487.61
		========
	Total	$40,000.39

Take an excel spread sheet and duplicate this with your salary. Or test the program John created for this calculation. If you get a windfall this large, this would be one way of creating your financial freedom. However, short of the lottery or a big inheritance, most people don't start out here.

If by chance you do receive a windfall, keeping the proceeds of it in a savings account for at least six months while you do a ton of research into your options would be at least one way of changing where your 'financial thermostat'** is set.

* Bank fees are not included in this illustration.

Secrets of the Millionaire Mind, **ISBN: 0060763280 T. Harv Eker

Real Estate Investing

Rental properties are another classic example of "Passive Income."

If you can buy a property (in addition to your home) and you can rent it out for more than you pay on its mortgage, then you have a rental property that is creating passive income.

This is a terrific way of creating passive income, but it is not the epitome of passive income.

There are risks - renters can do damage costing more money than you've made with the passive income stream. Some months the property might not be rented, turning the passive income property into a complete expense - possibly wiping out what you made to that point.

Is it time dependent? That depends on how urgent the current renter's needs are or how much repair needs to be done to get it to rental status. You don't work hourly at this job, but it can command quite a bit of your time.

Are you materially involved with it? Yes, to buy it up front, get the appraisal, determine the market, do the fix ups and be the landlord.

Can you walk away and still make money? Not really, the renter needs a landlord. Instead of calling this true passive income, it is more like opening a small business.

We have had a rental property before, but it never was one with a positive cash flow and even when we finally unloaded it, it was more trouble than it was worth.

However, many, many people have found this method the way to true freedom and if you have good credit and can get mortgages on rental properties that you can keep rented, then it is good "almost" passive income.

The income created from these properties can be used to create more passive income by keeping it in a savings account, CD or retirement account. Keep the money that comes in working for you or put it to work for you in as many ways as possible and you'll achieve the financial freedom you want sooner than you ever thought possible.

There are many good resources for real estate investing - check for the latest top 10 books on this topic at :

http://FindABookForMe.com/RealEstateInvesting.php

Stock Market

These types of investments are designed to grow your money in significant ways. Again, they are the epitome of passive income unless you decide to futz with them like a 'day trader.' If you do that, you've just given yourself another job. You might enjoy this job, but nevertheless, it's a job and not truly passive income.

Is it time dependent? Not usually, if you're in the market for the long haul. You might watch it, but you don't usually act upon the day to day happenings.

Are you materially involved with it? Again, not really, unless you like shuffling your money around from place to place, which most financial analysts will probably advise against. However... it is your money.

Can you walk away from it and have it still pay you money? Ultimately, yes, you sure can. It does all the work for you.

Is it risky?

Yes, more so than a bank, but many people have made fortunes here - and conversely, many people have lost everything here.

Without selling your stocks and creating a windfall, the only way the income is truly passive is if there are dividends sent to the stockholders.

We've owned stock and enjoyed the dividend checks and the money from their ultimate sale. We still own some utility stocks and receive an annual dividend check. The first stock was that of our employer at the time. We're not sure we would have bought it on the open market, without doing a heck of a lot more research. The second stock came with the house we own, again, much more a bonus than a conscious decision.

For the latest top 10 books on the subject of investing in the stock market, enter :

http://FindABookForMe.com/StockInvesting.php

Private Equity Investing

The stock market provides a way to invest in companies who have taken their ownership public. Private Equity Investing is investing in companies who have not 'IPO-ed' or 'gone public' yet.

This is the kind of investment that is at the highest risk to you, but they are also the ones with fantastic possible returns. So, if you decide to do this - you must do your research and decide if something this risky is for you. For most people, it is not. For most people, they don't even qualify to be able to invest in this type of venture - because they are not 'accredited investors.'* If you are not an accredited investor, you have to have a pre-existing relationship with the owners of the company that is raising capital.

Every now and again, an amazing offer comes through and the people who had the vision got very wealthy. Of course, the converse is also true - and the investor lost everything. Again, that is the nature of this beast. It's all about risk, reward and return.

* Accredited Investor - the basic definition varies from state to state, but the general definition is: a person who has at least a million dollars in net worth - without including their primary residence.

These ventures exist everywhere and are not always limited to the millionaires of the world. If you do end up with enough passive income just sitting in a bank and would like to play ***with a part of it*** in a high risk, high return venture, keep your eyes open for Private Equity Investments. These can not be advertised in the paper, so you need to know what kind of networking groups and training organizations exist to service these start-ups. If you get around these groups, the opportunities will literally fall at your feet. Again, however, this isn't something you bet the farm on - only a comfortable amount of the passive income you have coming in after your expenses. This has to be patient money, because it can sometimes take years to pay off.

The biggest part of this avenue of creating passive income - is that you must do your research, you must do your due diligence because the investment type is so high risk!

We recently invested in a small start up company (with amazing potential) and since it is an LLC (Limited Liability Corporation), we own membership units, not "stock." It has not paid us back for our investment in dividends yet, but we have been able to capitalize on our association with the company and made passive income on its products in other ways.

So, by the time the dividend checks do roll around, we'll have two sources of passive income from this company. Then when they ultimately sell, we'll have a great windfall check that will find a home where it can create more wonderful passive income for us.

To understand the science of getting rich is therefore the most essential of all knowledge.

There is nothing wrong in wanting to get rich.

The desire for riches is really the desire for a richer, fuller, and more abundant life; and that desire is praise worthy. The person who does not desire to live more abundantly is abnormal, and so the one who does not desire to have money enough to buy all they want is abnormal.

Wallace D. Waddles
The Science of Getting Rich
Published in 1910

Your Needs Your Goal

If you want to see things change, you have to do things you've never done before.

Calculate Your Expenses - Know Your Goal

We'll discuss housing, vehicle, grocery, debt and medical expenses and outline how to calculate their total on a monthly basis. What we are after is what your monthly expenses are and what they will need to be before you become financially free.

Several very important expenses to consider are the ones that your employer usually handles for you that you will have to pay for yourself as soon as you are financially free.

The first expense is taxes. Income taxes, state and local taxes, and self-employment taxes. Once you decide what your expenses are and what you will be earning, add a safe percentage to that to cover taxes. We suggest at least 25% to 30%. This might seem like a staggering number, but if you save more for taxes than you need, once you've paid taxes for the year, the rest is like getting a bonus back. Think of it as the "new way to get your tax refund!"

The second expense is insurance premiums including but not limited to medical, disability, dental and vision coverage. These expenses will no longer be taken out of your paycheck, you'll have to be sure you have a plan for obtaining coverage in these areas so that some problem doesn't overwhelm your budget and send you back into the workforce!

The last expense is a retirement account. Once you create passive income, you have created a way to get paid regardless of your age. However, it is imperative that you set some portion of your earnings aside and into some type of savings account. It'll be another security blanket and another form of passive income working to support you in your new *free life!*

HOUSING

Whether you rent or own your home, you have a housing expense. Even if you've paid off your home in full, you still have insurance and taxes. If you rent, you likely have renter's insurance, etc. You'll need to make improvements and repairs to your house at some time in any given year, so that expense is also included (as well as a suggested way of calculating it as a monthly expense if you've never broken it out like this). You should add housekeeping or landscaping expenses to the maintenance line.

Later on, we'll discuss where you could cut expenses to lower the ultimate amount of cash you'll need from month to month to initially reach your financial freedom goal. We've split out the following housing expenses thusly:

House Payment (P&I) or Rent____________________
House Payment (Taxes)_________________________
House Payment (Insurance)______________________

*House Maintenance ___________________________

*1% of the value of your house / 12 months
For example, a $250,000 house = $2,500/12 or $208.33.
(plus housekeeping or landscaping expenses)

Car Expenses

For each car list monthly expenses:

Payments ______________________________
Car Insurance ____________________________
Car Maintenance _________________________
Gas ___________________________________
*Other _________________________________

Payments ______________________________
Car Insurance ____________________________
Car Maintenance _________________________
Gas ___________________________________
*Other _________________________________

Payments ______________________________
Car Insurance ____________________________
Car Maintenance _________________________
Gas ___________________________________
*Other _________________________________

*List things under 'other' such as toll road charges or parking charges or commuting charges.

UTILITIES

Heat: ______________________________

Water: ______________________________

Electricity: ______________________________

Sewer: ______________________________

Homeowners Association: ______________________________

Phones: ______________________________

Cell Phone: ______________________________

TV: ______________________________

Internet: ______________________________

Other: ______________________________

____

____

Put a star by any of these items that you think you can substantially reduce or eliminate.

Put two stars by any item you think will increase due to circumstances beyond your control. For example, you might have to get a new cell phone because your child needs it, or the cost of heating your house is rising or some contractual increase on your cable bill is coming up.

DEBT

List the interest rate, current balance and usual monthly payment* for each one of these debt sources that you have. Don't list your house or car payments, they are already included in this calculation.

Credit Card ______________________________

Credit Card ______________________________

Credit Card ______________________________

Credit Card ______________________________

Bank Loan ______________________________

Bank Loan ______________________________

Family Loan ____________________________

Friend Loan ____________________________

Medical Bill _____________________________

Medical Bill _____________________________

Medical Bill _____________________________

Other: ________________________________

* Usual payment is the one you usually pay each month. If it varies, write in the amount that you think you'll need to pay to keep these current.

Health Insurance

For most people, health insurance premiums come out of their paycheck. If you're financially free, you'll be responsible for the insurance premium and all the co-pays as well as any previously incurred debt you enter your financial freedom with. Keep this in mind when figuring your freedom number.

Other health related expenses might be a weekly massage or nutritional supplements you like to take.

Medical Premium ____________________
Dental Premium ____________________
Vision Premium ____________________
Short Term Disability ____________________
Long Term Disability ____________________
Life Insurance ____________________

Medical Payments ____________________
(Tally up what you spent last year and average it over the 12 months (by dividing it by 12) to get a monthly expense figure.

Other: ____________________

____

ALL THE REST

Groceries ______________________________

School Expenses ________________________

Do you have school aged children? You'll have to consider their annual registration and book fees and set aside some money for it.

Child Support __________________________

Other Monthly Expenses ______________

____

____

____

____

____

* We can't anticipate everything - you know what your bills are. List them here so you truly know what your ultimate goal amount will be.

TOTAL IT UP!

Monthly Housing ______________________________

Monthly Cars ______________________________

Monthly Utilities ______________________________

Monthly Debt ______________________________

Monthly Insurance______________________________

Monthly All The Rest______________________________

Total Before Taxes ______________________________

Taxes * ______________________________

Grand Total
Monthly Expenses ______________________________

* Multiply the Total Before Taxes by 25% - enter that number for Taxes.

The grand total is your **financial freedom goal amount**. If you can get your total passive income or your non-job income up to and past this number, you are financially free.

Pep Talk!

Write your financial freedom goal amount here!

____

How does that number feel to you - too high perhaps?

Are you meeting it with the job(s) you're already doing? Some of us are strapped so tight right now, the answer might be no. So the need to create another income stream or two is essential.

If you listen to the financially free people - ones who have already achieved what you want to achieve - they will tell you to set a goal. They will tell you to set a really, really big goal, often times, something that feels ridiculously big. ***If that's how that number feels to you - then that is actually good news!***

Take a deep breath!!!

If you are going to travel this path to financial freedom, then you have to first believe it is possible. And if you choose to get started and do something new to create passive income, it is really possible.

Once you create a little passive income, you'll realize you can create a lot. Then this target number won't seem so big or scary, it'll merely be a goal, and once you reach it - you'll really have accomplished something spectacular!

Go for it!!!

Create win/win opportunities. There is enough money to go around and around again!

Can You Decrease Your Expenses Anywhere?

Now, having said that your personal financial freedom goal amount is nothing to be afraid of, let's see if it is at all adjustable. You need to look closely at all your expense entries to re-evaluate where each number originally came from and decide if there is some way that you can reduce the amount.

You'll probably be successful at reducing many of these expenses. So, we suggest putting these entries into a spreadsheet program, and as you find ways to reduce the expenses, you can also reduce your financial freedom goal amount.

This number will probably fluctuate with your situation. Keep as accurate a number as possible in front of you at all times. Track your progress "growing income" as well as "reducing expenses." Do it at least every month, and keep it in front of you, but don't re-evaluate it too often, because then you'll be obsessing about these numbers instead of using that energy to create ideas and passive income streams!

Should You Increase Your Expenses Temporarily?

This may sound contradictory to what we've been discussing to this point, but right now we have to think about your current resources and apply that against your potential new income and future financial freedom.

The questions to ask yourself might be:

Should you hire a housekeeper for three months so that you free up more time to write your book?

Should you hire an accountant to do your taxes, so that you free up a bunch of time right away?

Should you hire a landscaper or even a teenager to keep your yard up while you use your talents to create some things to sell?

Do these trade offs of money for your time make sense in the short run, so that they can really pay off for you in the long run? You need to assess your availability to your own future.

Vacations

You will notice that we didn't have you budget in a vacation in your passive income budget. The reason for that is, if you don't have to work anymore, *there's a really good chance you are not going to work anymore.* So to schedule a 'vacation' doesn't make any sense.

However, you need to enjoy your new life, or you will find a way to 'have' to go back to the old way, so remember to do fun things while you're off of work.

If you choose to continue to work, even after you are financially free, then you should have enough money to take a vacation whenever and wherever you want to go.

The goal is to increase your income to exceed expenses and vacation expense doesn't make sense to include in the freedom calculation.

Just remember to have fun once you're financially free - and all will be well with your world!

How Much Income Do You Bring in Right Now?

Job #1: ______________________________

Job #2: ______________________________

Job #3: ______________________________

Child Support ______________________________

Other ______________________________

Other ______________________________

Other ______________________________

Other ______________________________

* Star any that are passive income streams.

Create Your Plan

If you're like most people, you actually already have a start on developing your passive income, you just never thought about it in this sense before.

If you labeled anything passive income in the prior step, can you do more of it? If not, ask yourself, is it a time-sink and should you let it go to actively pursue some other avenues of passive income?

Your time initially creating the plan, the ideas, doing the writing or the research is critical right now. You need to decide if what you are doing is worth your very valuable time. If so, by all means, keep doing it. If not, cut it down or cut it out.

Now that you have done all the exercises in this book - ask yourself, what idea appealed to me the most? Then list your top three options. Create a cost-benefit analysis or estimated expense-to-income sheet.

Then ask yourself, can you afford to do this using your current talents and resources? If so, go for it. If not, ask yourself how you can test the waters with this? Is there a way to partially do it or to start small and build up to the ultimate goal?

These questions are critical when deciding your next few action steps.

If the answer is that you can't afford to do it, but it is so brilliant you really want to give it a try, explore the option of using someone else's money. Can you get a loan from a bank, a friend or a new business partner? Create a win/win. Offer to pay the friend back in interest higher than the bank would pay AND offer him/her a perpetual percentage of your profits. Create a win/win and watch how quickly someone in your circle of influence steps up to help you with your idea.

If you don't have the funding and can't find it for some reason, table that idea for the moment and work on another idea that doesn't involve any start up capital. Then when you have that idea bringing in some passive income, it could fuel your original favorite idea.

The goal is to diversify. The idea is to make your resources work for you. There are so many ways to do it, the options are staggering.

The secret is to begin.

Go for it - and some day soon, you'll be "livin' the free life!"

Conclusion

Ultimately, you have to create your own destiny, come up with your own ideas, do your own due diligence and get it going.

This book is called "Secrets To Creating Passive Income" and we've already revealed the real secret and that is to begin. You have to choose the free life and find the tools that will make it real for you.

We've given you an amazing set of resources. But you are your best resource. Give it some thought, understand how possible becoming financially free is and then go for it.

Our favorite saying of late is, "At the moment of commitment, the universe conspires to assist you." So, commit to yourself because you have all the tools it takes to set yourself and your family free!

May you live long and prosper!

Challenge

Ten dollars a day might not sound like much, but over the course of a year it adds up quickly - to $3650.

Researching CD accounts online *(5 months with a $5000 minimum deposit)*, the interest rate of return was 3.1%. To make $10/day, you need $117,741.93 in the account to start.

It is much easier to make $10/day doing something that you love instead of waiting for your money to grow in a bank. Apply the following interest formula to any passive income that you earn. Determine how much you would have to have held in the bank to make the same amount daily *(non-compounded)*.

You'll probably have a wide range of emotions when you see the dollar amounts, we hope one of them is a feeling of affluence.

For example, here's how to calculate the amount of money you'd have to have in the bank to earn $10 daily at today's rates in passive interest income. ***Multiply the daily amount by 365 then divide that quantity by the interest rate.***

$10 /day at 3.1%'s formula is:

(10 * 365) / (3.1/100) = $117,741.93

or

(10 * 365) / .031 = $117, 741.93*

It has been said that an extra $300/month would avert 90% of the bankrupcies in this country. An extra $10/day or $300/month does change lives.

Using the 3.1% interest rate model, another magic number is $84.94. If you could make this amount of money per day, it would be the same as having $1,000,000 in the bank making 3.1% income. We call this reaching the "**Passivillionaire**™" level.

This is an extra $31,000+ a year in income. Would that change your life? We hope this information helps you reach the passivillionaire level this year and surpass it greatly from that point on.

To your prosperity!

Pass It On

Once you are able to become financially free yourself, teach others to do it too. There are enough different ways to create financial abundance that everyone can do it. The beauty of this way of creating income is all of the win/win scenarios created. No one need be left behind, this doesn't have to happen at the 'cost' of anyone else.

Turn the people you care about on to this book or make them partners in your ventures or just plain teach them from your experience.

Everyone hopes their children will end up being better off that they are, what better skill to teach them than the path to financial freedom?

The old competitive model is giving way to the new cooperative model. The cooperative approach to business creates allies, partners, team and benefactors and the rate of growth of these types of ventures far out-performs those created using the competitive models.

Create the win/win situations, teach others. There is enough to go around, so pass it on!

SOURCES & RESOURCES

Recommended Books:

Advanced Book Marketing **0-9820838-6-6** EJ Thornton
Angel On Board **1-932344-76-4** EJ Thornton
Revenue Beyond Royalties **1-932344-39-X** EJ Thornton
Secrets of the Millionaire Mind **0060763280** T. Harv Eker
So You Want To Write A Book **0-9801941-3-X** Othniel J. Seiden
The Basics of Profitable Publishing, **1-932344-50-0** EJ Thornton
The Science of Getting Rich by Wallace Waddles ForTheWealthOfAll.com
Rethinking Retirement by Keith Weber, EarlyRetirementHelp.com

Interesting Books:

Visual Basic 2005 Cookbook **0596101775** John Craig & Tim Patrick
Visual Basic 6.0 Developers Workshop, **157231883X** John Craig
Health and the Domino Effect **1932344551** Sharon Price, CN
What Will Set You Free **0-9774761-8-9** Cynthia James
Brother Asaiah, **0-9779960-4-2** Martha Ellen Anderson
Sex in the Golden Years **0-9801941-0-5** Othniel J. Seiden, MD & Jane Bilett, Ph.D.
The Second Half Begins at 50 **0-9801941-1-3** Othniel J. Seiden, MD & Jane Bilett, Ph.D.
Heavy & Healthy **0-9779960-5-0** Othniel J. Seiden, MD & Jane Bilett, Ph.D.

Tele-seminars:

How to Publish your book by EJ Thornton: EJThornton.com

Seven Ways To Make Everyday a Payday by EJ Thornton ForTheWealthOfAll.com

Resource Websites:

AdvancedBookMarketing.com
AssociatedContent.com
BooksToBelieveIn.com
BoomerBookSeries.com
Clickbank.com
EJThornton.com
E-lance.com
Examiner.com
FindABookForMe.com/RealEstateInvesting.php
FindABookForMe.com/StockInvesting.php
FreeConferenceCalling.com
ForTheWealthOfAll.com
FreeU.com
Hartunian.com
RevenueBeyond.com
ShawGuides.com
ThorntonPublishing.com
JohnClarkCraig.com
WritersSummit.com/Articles.php
WritersSummit.com/AffiliatePrograms.php
WritersSummit.com/IntellectualProperty.php
WritersSummit.com/PrivateEquityInvesting.php
WritersSummit.com/Publishing.php
WritersSummit.com/WebOptimization.php
WritersToBelieveIn.com/THarvEker.php

Examples, Interesting & Fun Websites
Cloudbait.com
CNN.com
Heavens-Above.com
LucidLights.net
LucidBrake.com
PetHealthFocus.com
Sports-Top-10.com
Sun-Track.com

Affiliate Programs:
AffilloBluePrint.com
Amazon.com
asseenontv.com
ClickBank.com
CommissionJunction.com
Ebay.com
Google.com/adsense

Foresite Websites:
GreatAngelBooks.com
GreatRelationshipBooks.com
DogCancerBooks.com
EarlyRetirementHelp.com
DogLoverBooks.com
InvestingAdviceBooks.com
NostalgicNovels.com
GreatMemoirs.com
SpeakingWithTheSpirits.com
TrueHopeBooks.com
SurvivingInfidelity.com
RevenueBeyond.com

To Your Prosperity!

Order Form
Secrets To Creating Passive Income

$24.95 + 3.50 (S&H)

online at: http://RevenueBeyond.com

by phone: (303) 794-8888

by fax: (720) 863-2013

by mail:
send check payable to:
Thornton Publishing, Inc.
17011 Lincoln Ave. #408
Parker, Colorado 80134

If it is temporarily sold out at your favorite bookstore,
have them order more of ISBN: 0-9801941-9-9

Name: ______________________________
Address: ______________________________
____
Phone: ______________________________
E-mail: ______________________________

Credit Card #: ______________________________
Card Type: ____________ Expiration Date: ____/ ____
Security Code: ________